Transphobia

Deal with it
and be
a gender
transcender

j wallace skelton • Illustrated by Nick Johnson

James Lorimer & Company Ltd., Publishers
Toronto

In gym class, the girls' track team is arguing with the coach. "He's not a real girl," one of the sprinters yells. "It's unfair to have him try out for our team when he is stronger and faster."

Later, you see a student being blocked from going in the boys' washroom. Two big guys stand shoulder to shoulder in front of the door so he can't get past. They tell him that since he's only dressed like a boy, he has to go somewhere else.

What's going on here?
Both are examples of transphobia.

Transphobia is based on a series of ideas many people have about sex and gender — about people being boys or girls. Some people bully, exclude, or act unfairly to people they think don't match these ideas. That's transphobia. When they insist that people live up to these ideas, and punish those who don't, that's transphobia too.

No matter what gender you are, this book can help you think about transphobia and make more room for more people to express who they are.

Contents

Transphobia 101   4
The Gender Explorer   14
The Gender Enforcer   20
The Witness   26
More Help   32

What is Transphobia?

Transphobia is when actions and attitudes are based on certain assumptions:

- everyone is either male or female

- all males are masculine

- all females are feminine

- there is no way to change sex or gender

- you can tell what sex someone is by the way they look

- people who don't match these assumptions are somehow bad or wrong

But what about:

- people who know they are a sex other than what they were identified as at birth?

- people who don't identify as a boy or a girl?

- people who can't be easily identified as female or male?

- boys and men who are seen as "too feminine" — even sometimes?

- women and girls who are seen as "too butch" — even sometimes?

That's a lot of people who are laughed at, teased, avoided, excluded, threatened, or targeted because of transphobia! Transphobia is not trusting someone to tell us what sex or gender they are, when, really, we all should get to be our own experts. Nobody knows you better than you!

Transphobia is based on

certain kinds of thinking...

Transphobia 101
QUIZ

Transphobic or Not?

Transphobia demands that we all have to live up to stereotypes of what it means to be female or male. It means people are discriminated against for being who they are. Check out the following and answer which are transphobic and which are not.

1 Mr./Ms. Messed Up

For the debate competition, students will be introduced as Ms. or Mr. with their last names. Lake asks, "What about those of us who aren't either, or are both?" Lake is told to choose one.

Yes. It's transphobic to insist that everyone is either a Ms. or a Mr. This denies many non-binary people their preferred title.

2 Elected Official

While running for student council president, Jaleel comes out as trans. Jaleel wins by a landslide. His opponent Nayeema says it's because everyone feels sorry for Jaleel.

Yes. It's transphobic to assume that Jaleel won for being trans. Students could have voted for this candidate for many reasons.

3 The Facts Don't Lie

Isabel would like to sign up for Girls' Club after school. The people running the club tell her she has to bring her birth certificate to prove she's a girl.

Maybe. If they ask only the girls they think are trans, then this is transphobic. If they ask everyone, it's not intentionally transphobic, although still a barrier.

4 Picture Perfect

The photographer gives your graduating class the following instructions: "Everyone should wear a gown for graduation. Boys will hold a diploma, and girls will hold a rose."

No. It's sexist, but it's not transphobic.

5 Spreading the News

You tell your friend that you'd like to ask out Kal. Your friend says that, since he used to be a girl, going out with him would make you a lesbian.

Yes. This is transphobic, homophobic, and spreading rumours all at the same time.

6 On the List

When you register for school, you can put down whatever name you want the school to use. But you can only change it once a year.

No. Being able to choose their name on the attendance list will make things easier and safer for trans students.

7 Door Number One

The community centre has one change room for girls and one for boys. Lu, who identifies as non-binary, asks for a space to change. Lu is told, "We can't make a change room just for you!"

Yes. The community centre needs to serve the whole community, including Lu.

8 Online Ranking

Nikki (who used to be Nick) posts her picture to a site where people rank hotness and leave comments. She gets low hotness scores and lots of comments about how to look "more like a girl."

Yes. This is sexist and transphobic.

9 Easy A

You're choosing classes for high school. Your big brother tells you to ask for Mr. Bird for history. "He used to be a girl, and he still marks easy, like a woman."

Yes and no. It's not transphobic to want to be in Mr. Bird's class. Your brother's reason is sexist. Outing Mr. Bird as trans though, that might be transphobic.

10 Don't Know

Your parents tell you that they don't know any trans people.

No. It's not transphobic, but it's probably wrong. They just don't know anyone who has shared that they are trans with them.

Dear Conflict Counsellor

Q: On my football team, there's a guy who used to be a girl. Some people say he shouldn't be using the boys' change room. How can I help my team?

— Team Player

A: It doesn't matter who someone used to be — what's important is who they are now. Not allowing one player into the change room because of who he used to be is discrimination. And it's bad for team morale. Showing you support for this player and standing up for him will help make the change room a safer place for everyone. And that's teamwork!

Q: I don't know if someone's a boy or a girl. Is it okay to ask?

— *Wants to Know*

A: Maybe. If you have no reason to ask except curiosity, it's not polite to ask. If you are going to be introducing this person, or they are part of your class or community, it's probably polite to respectfully ask what pronouns they prefer. Ask once, making sure the person won't be embarrassed in front of others. Or you can just use the person's name instead of he/she/them.

Q: If a person is trans, does that mean they are gay?

— *Straightening it Out*

A: Nope. Knowing that a person is trans does not tell you anything about who they are attracted to. Being trans is about a person's gender or sex. Being gay is about their sexual orientation. Like cis people — who identify as the sex they were assigned when they were born — trans people can be straight, lesbian, gay, bisexual, asexual, queer, or questioning.

Q: Other girls in my class are shaving their legs and changing their clothes. They've said that I need to do that too, or I can't be their friend anymore. I don't want to — does that mean I'm trans?

— *Questioning Identity*

A: Being trans has to do with your identity, not the clothes you wear or whether you shave your legs. Girls can shave their legs (or not) and wear whatever they want to, and still be girls. A boy can shave his legs, and it doesn't make him any less of a boy. On the other hand, if you find yourself thinking, "I don't want to shave my legs; that's a girl thing and I'm not a girl," you may be trans. But it's not the shaving — it's the part where you identify as something other than the sex you were assigned at birth.

Myths

You can always tell who is trans.

Some trans people choose to keep their trans status to themselves. Others loudly proclaim that they are trans. You can't always tell by looking.

People who are trans know from a very young age.

Some people do, and some people don't. There is no one "right time" to figure out questions of identity. And that's true for all of us.

STUDENT

NAME: BLANK, MEL
SEX: F   AGE : 13

MBlank

People always have their true sex and their real name on their ID.

A person's "true sex" is how they identify themselves. A person's "real name" is the name that feels real to them, regardless of what's on their ID.

DID YOU KNOW?

- It's estimated that 1 in 500 people are transsexual.

Single-sex washrooms are safer for everyone than "all-gender" ones.

Washrooms are safe when nobody in them behaves in ways that are unsafe, threatening, harassing, policing, or dangerous. It's not whether it's "single-sex" or "all-gender" — it's what people do inside them.

Trans is a new thing.

The word "trans" might be recent, but people in all cultures and across history have taken on gender roles other than what we might expect based on their sex.

All people transition the same way.

Transition is the process of changing from one identity category to another. There is no one way to transition, as there is no one way to be trans.

• At least 130 of the First Nations had two-spirit roles before the arrival of Europeans on Turtle Island. Many still do.

• In the 1950s, '60s and '70s, "men dressed in women's clothing" were arrested and detained or charged.

The **Gender Explorer**

You know who you are!

Maybe you don't think of yourself as a girl or boy, but as both — or neither. Maybe you're sure you are a girl, even if that's not what other people have always expected. Maybe you are sure you're a boy, even though your birth certificate says female. Maybe you are a tomboy, or you're a boy who likes wearing dresses.

There are lots of ways to have a gender!

DEAR DR. SHRINK-WRAPPED...

Q: I wore a dress and make-up to school for Halloween as a costume — and looked really great. Since then, random people have been asking if it means I really want to be a girl. Some kids have even started teasing and picking on me. How do I prove to them I'm really happy being a guy?
— *Glad to Be a Guy*

A: Hey, Glad, you know who you are, and that's what's important. If the people asking/teasing/harassing you have jumped to conclusions about your identity, you shouldn't have to prove anything to them. Dr. Shrink-Wrapped suggests you ask them to stop. Their behaviour is transphobic, and that's a problem for everyone. If asking them to stop does not end the questions and bullying, you might decide to make a complaint to the school and have an adult address their transphobic behaviour.

Q: It's like the whole world is divided into things for girls and things for boys: washrooms, change rooms, sports teams, health class — even pronouns! I identify as non-binary. I don't feel I should have to choose to be a boy or girl. The pronouns that feel best for me are they/them. People keep telling me I have to group myself with the girls, and they use she/her for me. How do I make sure there is room — and a pronoun — for me?

— *Just Call Me Neither*

A: Dr. Shrink-Wrapped hears you, Just! Our culture assumes that we can all be divided into two neat groups, and everything has been set up that way. You are not the only person this does not work for! You have rights, and your non-binary identity deserves respect. But you might need to ask and make complaints about the lack of non-gendered spaces and groups to make change. You also might have to educate people. Tell people that they/them is not always plural. Tell them that lots of the authors you study in English class — such as Austen, Dickens, and Shakespeare — and most dictionaries okay these words as singular personal pronouns.

The **Gender Explorer**

QUIZ

When you encounter transphobia, how do you respond?

Do you Speak Up and clearly state what you need? Do you go on the offensive and Flare Up? Or do you Put Up with transphobic behaviour? Step up and take this quiz to find out.

I Speak Up

I Put Up

I Flare Up

1 You're waiting for the bus. Someone you don't know very well starts to ask you questions about trans identities. You don't mind answering the first one, but the questions keep coming and the bus doesn't. You feel less and less comfortable answering, so you . . .

a) Keep answering the questions because, hey, he's got to learn somewhere.

b) Say, "I need to take a break from answering these questions. I could suggest some good books and websites for you to look up the rest."

c) Say, "I can't believe you are asking me all this — what do you think I am, Wikipedia? Stop. Just stop."

a) Put Up   b) Speak Up   c) Flare Up

---

2 You asked your friends to call you by a new name and use "he" instead of "she" when they talk about you. One of your friends says "The name's not a problem, but I'm not going to call you **he** until I know you've had the surgery." What do you do?

a) You say, "As a friend, I need you to do better. Respect me and use my new name and pronoun."

b) You shout, "You're going to judge me based on what you imagine about a part of my body you've never seen? What kind of friend are you?!"

c) You roll your eyes and walk away.

a) Speak Up   b) Flare Up   c) Put Up

---

3 At a friend's sleepover, she tells you, "I don't want your being trans to make people uncomfortable. You can sleep in my room." When you find out the rest of them will be in sleeping bags in the basement, you say . . .

a) "I feel really uncomfortable with being segregated. Let's find a way we can all stay together."

b) Nothing. Later, you pretend to have a stomach ache and go home.

c) "It's totally insulting to make me sleep somewhere else. If you were really my friend you wouldn't ask that."

a) Speak Up   b) Put Up   c) Flare Up

---

4 There's a classmate you're really into, so you ask to spend time together. You watch a movie together at your place, and talk until 3 a.m. But then she says, "I really like you, but please don't tell anyone at school. I don't want people to know I'm dating a trans person." How do you respond?

a) You slam the door and promise to never talk to her again.

b) You say, "I'm not comfortable dating someone who can't be open about our relationship. Let me know if you can be okay with it, or if we should just be friends."

c) You say, "It's okay, the only thing that matters is how it is when we're together."

a) Flare Up   b) Speak Up   c) Put Up

---

5 At your doctor's office, you tell the receptionist that you now use the name "Jenny" and ask him to change the name on your file. At your appointment time, you hear him call out, "Jethro? Jethro? Jethro? JETHRO?" Do you . . .

a) Get up and go in to see the doctor?

b) Ignore him, wait an hour, and then loudly complain how unfair it is you have never been called?

c) Say to the receptionist, "Excuse me, is it my turn? I think I was called, but I'm not sure because you did not use my new name."?

a) Put Up   b) Flare Up   c) Speak Up

---

6 You're able-bodied, but the only washroom that feels safe to you is the accessible washroom — the only all-gender one. A group of kids see you leaving it and start asking loudly, "Hey, how come you're using that washroom? What's wrong with you?" They start following you down the hall, shouting at you. You know you have to report this to the school, but what else do you do?

a) You go back in the washroom, close the door, and wait for them to leave.

b) You yell angrily, "A hell of a lot less than is wrong with you!"

c) You say "Nothing!" and walk off.

a) Put Up   b) Flare Up   c) Speak Up

---

7 You identify as a boy, but you happen to like doing things people say are "girly." You want to join the knitting club and take home economics. But some girls say that having you there would make them uncomfortable. And the boys have started to call you a sissy. How do you react?

a) You sign up for carpentry and join the gaming club instead.

b) You sneak into the school to tangle up the knitting club's yarn and paint graffiti in the home-ec kitchen. That will show them you're a guy!

c) You explain to the girls that you're just there to knit and learn to cook, and that there are no rules against guys trying to learn useful skills.

a) Put Up   b) Flare Up   c) Speak Up

---

8 There's a rumour going around school that the new boy is really a girl. You hear some of your classmates say that they are going to corner him in the washroom and pull down his pants so they can know for sure. You know you have to report bullying to the school, and you also

a) Shout, "You're going to assault the new kid? What are you thinking?"

b) Offer to go to the washroom with the new student. If the other kids try anything, you can speak up or go get help.

c) Do nothing. It's not your business because you're not involved.

a) Flare Up   b) Put Up   c) Speak Up

---

9 You need your student card to get the student rate on the bus, but you were D'Shawn and now you're Denise. You go to get a new photo taken, but the staff person tells you they have a "no retakes" policy. What do you do?

a) You call the staff person transphobic and walk away.

b) You take the card and walk away. You'll get a new one next year.

c) You explain that you are trans, and you want a new card to match your new identity.

a) Flare Up   b) Put Up   c) Speak Up

---

10 You find out that your best friend invited a bunch of people for a swim party on the weekend, but didn't include you. What do you do?

a) Nothing. You can't invite everyone all the time.

b) You tell your other friends how much your best friend hurt your feelings and ask them never to hang out with her again.

c) You tell your friend how you feel and ask why you weren't invited.

a) Put Up   b) Flare Up   c) Speak Up

Keeping Track

Use these basic tools to help protect yourself and those around you from transphobia.

Know your rights
If you know your rights, it's easier to feel empowered and easier to make sure other people treat you right. Look up the human rights code of your province or territory and other laws that protect you. Most organizations, clubs, and schools have equity or human rights policies too!

Find resources
Sometimes other people don't do the right thing because they don't know what the right thing is. Look for books, pamphlets, websites, and other resources you feel good about. Read them and offer to share them with others. Sometimes a book or a pamphlet can be a good conversation-starter.

Be clear about what you need
If you meet with someone about changing things, don't arrive with just a bunch of problems. Have a list of what you want written out in point-form. It's easier for someone to say yes to a solution you are proposing than to have to guess what might work.

Find allies
It's easier to fight discrimination and make change with allies. Allies don't have to be people who experience the discrimination, but they are people who care and are willing to back you up. Allies can also help you problem solve, de-stress, and feel better about who you are.

DID YOU KNOW?

• The Canadian Human Rights Commission says that you cannot be discriminated against because of your gender. That includes gender identity.

dos and don'ts

✓ Do know that you are precious and valuable exactly as you are.

✓ Do decide who to tell and who not to tell.

✓ Do decide if, how, and when you transition.

✓ Do ask for people to call you by the right name and pronoun.

✓ Do find supportive adults around you and talk with them.

✓ Do get help if people harass you, disrespect you, or make you feel unsafe!

✓ Do find out where the single-stall washrooms are in buildings you use often.

✓ Do find other people with similar identities.

✓ Do keep yourself safe.

✗ Don't be hard on yourself for not responding to transphobia.

✗ Don't answer questions that make you feel uncomfortable.

✗ Don't be afraid to ask for what you need.

✗ Don't assume that adults are always right.

✗ Don't feel responsible for speaking for all trans people.

✗ Don't feel pressure to look or dress a certain way.

Connect with supportive adults

Find adults who have your back. They may know about or be able to access information or services. If you want to report transphobia at school, to the police, or elsewhere, it's helpful to know which adults in the system will support you.

Care for yourself

You matter. Take time to look after you. Do things you enjoy. Do things that relax you, and things that help you get tension out of your body. Dealing with discrimination can cause anxiety, stress, and depression, so taking care of yourself is an important way to stand up to transphobia!

• The first person in Canada to argue that they must be a man because they had been living as a man was Jacques Lafargue, in 1738.

• One in ten elementary students report that people sometimes think their behaviour or appearance does not conform to traditional norms.

The **Gender Enforcer**

GIRLS LOCKER ROOM

You're not a transphobic, are you?

It's just that you know girls and boys are different, and they can do different things.

It's not rocket science!

You can't change the way things are — and if people can't fit in, there must be something wrong with them, right?

dos and don'ts

- ✓ Do question your assumptions about sex and gender.

- ✓ Do question gender stereotypes.

- ✓ Do challenge yourself to overcome prejudice against people who might be trans.

- ✓ Do think about how gender stereotypes limit everyone.

- ✓ Do respect everyone's right to decide who they are.

- ✓ Do listen when someone tells you who they are.

- ✓ Do ask people respectfully for the right name, pronouns, and identity to use for them.

- ✓ Do look beyond what a person is wearing to get to know the person inside.

- ✗ Don't let stereotypes limit what activities or classes you try.

- ✗ Don't assume that everyone is a boy or a girl, a man or a woman.

- ✗ Don't decide what someone's identity is based on what they are wearing.

- ✗ Don't make fun of people for not meeting your standards of femininity or masculinity.

- ✗ Don't use the word tranny.

- ✗ Don't assume that everyone has to be like you.

- ✗ Don't assume that someone is in the wrong washroom.

- ✗ Don't let other people tease, harass, or make fun of people because of their gender identity or gender expression.

- ✗ Don't demand that someone answer all your questions.

The **Gender Enforcer**

Are you a transphobic?

You don't even know anyone who's trans. And if you did, you wouldn't be phobic or afraid of them. But think about how assumptions and stereotypes can cause hurt and upset for others. Take the quiz to see how you measure up!

Are the following statements True or False?

1. I think there are only two genders, and you're born into one or the other.

2. To be respected, girls should look and act like girls, and boys should look and act like boys.

3. If I can't tell if someone is a man or a woman, it really bothers me.

4. I don't think it's possible for people to be a gender other than male or female.

5. I think that toys and clothing can be categorized as boys' and girls'.

6. I've seen kids being picked on for being a "sissy" boy or "tomboy" girl and said nothing.

7. I try to conform to gender stereotypes.

8. I think it's okay to make fun of people who don't conform to gender stereotypes.

9. I won't use an all-gender washroom.

10. I wouldn't have a trans friend.

11. There's nothing I can do about transphobia.

12. I've been accused of transphobia.

13. I think the sight of a man in a dress is funny.

14. I have laughed at jokes about trans people.

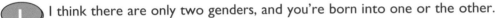

I have told jokes about trans people.

 I won't use "they" or "them" as a pronoun for one person.

 I challenge anyone I think might be in the wrong washroom for their sex.

I think is right for them (men's or women's).

If someone asks me for directions to the washroom, I only tell them how to get to the one I think is right for them (men's or women's).

 Trans people shouldn't be teachers or work with children.

 I have the right to judge other people.

I don't think that trans women and trans girls should be able to use a washroom with other women and girls.

 I don't think trans women should be able to compete in women's sports.

 I don't think the term "woman" includes trans women.

 I think that people who are transitioning should always take hormones.

 I think that people who are transitioning should always have surgery.

 I think that if you were born with a certain body, it's wrong to change it.

 I think gender affirmation surgery (used to be called a sex change or sex reassignment surgery) should be paid for by the person, not by society.

 If I see or hear people being transphobic, I don't do or say anything.

 I don't think we should be learning about sex and gender in school.

 I think there are more trans people because kids are learning about sex and gender too young.

How many **True answers** did you get? If there were a lot, you might have more to learn about **sex, gender, gender stereotypes, trans people, and transphobia.** Your beliefs and opinions could be making it harder for people around you. **Learning more may help!**

The Gender Enforcer

It's your choice!

You have to make sure that gender explorers don't ruin it for all of us, **right? Wrong.** Sometimes the beliefs we think are protecting us are actually limiting our choices. There are things you can do to make sure people around you **have more choices and possibilities.**

Choice of style
It's your job to figure out how to express your own style, and nobody else's. Don't feel limited by other people's assumptions and stereotypes. Experiment to figure out what makes you look and feel great. And celebrate everyone's choice of style.

Choice of behaviour
It's probably not possible to stop making assumptions. But we can question them and decide not to act on them. Ask yourself — would you be acting that way if that boy was a girl, or that girl was a boy? After thinking about it, try to treat every person the way you would like to be treated. Now that's an easy choice, isn't it?

Choice of impact
It's not enough to have good intentions, we need to think about what impact our words and actions might have on others. How might someone else judge you on what you are doing or saying?

When Safety Is Involved

Most of us deal with the kind of transphobia that makes everyday things difficult, unfair, and unpleasant. But it's important to know that transphobia can also take the form of violence.

The modern GLBTQ movement in North America began when trans women and cross dressers started fighting back against police violence. Amnesty International views people arrested or imprisoned for their sexual orientation or gender identity as political prisoners and works to free them.

Transphobia can be deadly. Many of the people killed by transphobic violence are young trans women of colour. It's never possible to address just one form of discrimination at a time — they often overlap. These groups are often victims of violence:

- young people
- people of colour
- women
- people living in poverty

The TransPulse Study found that transphobia actually affects the physical health of trans people. Living in transphobic environments can lead to higher rates of substance use, suicide, and depression for trans people than in the general population. It's not that being trans makes people suicidal. It's being discriminated against, devalued, disrespected, and made unsafe that can lead to stress, anxiety, and depression.

If someone you know is the victim of transphobic violence or might be thinking about suicide, it's important to get them help. Even if the person asks you to keep it confidential, it's important not to do that. Tell a safe adult so they can get help. Remember, doing that could save their life, and that's more important than keeping any secret.

Choice of language
You wouldn't like it if people always called you by your hated middle name. Always talk about a person using words that feel good to them. Get a person's name right, get their pronouns right, and use identity words you know they use. Don't share information about a person's trans status unless they have specifically told you it's okay to tell other people. Be respectful with your words.

Choice of assumptions
Think about what would happen if we got to know people as individuals, rather than relying on our assumptions about them. Instead of making assumptions, focus on asking respectful questions.

- Trans students have repeatedly identified washrooms and change rooms as the least safe places at school.

- 57 per cent of trans Ontarians report having avoided public washrooms because of their trans status.

The **Witness**

Have you seen someone be bullied or harassed because of the way they look or dress?

Have you heard people saying that someone is "trans" in a negative way or told they are "not really a girl" or "not really a boy"?

Did you want to do something?

Why didn't you?

26

You can transform your world

There are things you can do to make things safer and more welcoming for people around you. You can help others be more respectful and understanding. **Speaking up can be challenging**, but in the long run will make things better for everyone.

- Ask questions
- Challenge assumptions
- Be welcoming and friendly
- Stand up for your own rights
- Stand up for the rights of others
- Connect with others with similar goals

The strongest protections against transphobia come from human rights legislations. The Government of Canada, and provincial and territorial governments all offer protections. In Canada, discrimination because of gender identity or gender expression is not allowed and can be legally challenged.

Things don't get better on their own — it takes work!

dos and don'ts

✓ Do report transphobia and other forms of discrimination to a safe adult.

✓ Do speak up when you hear people expressing gender stereotypes.

✓ Do question gender segregation.

✓ Do recognize and challenge your own stereotypes about sex and gender.

✓ Do learn about different genders, gender identities, and gender expressions.

✓ Do join groups that target transphobia, homophobia, and gender stereotypes at school.

✓ Do start a group if your school does not have one.

✓ Do treat everyone with dignity and respect.

✓ Do be vocal in your support.

✗ Don't stay silent if you hear someone being targeted.

✗ Don't laugh at transphobia, homophobia, or other forms of discrimination.

✗ Don't speak on behalf of a targeted group you are not a part of.

✗ Don't respond with other kinds of prejudice.

✗ Don't assume you know how someone identifies without them telling you.

27

The Witness

QUIZ

Do you really get it?

So you know transphobia is wrong. The next time you witness it you know what you have to do. But do you really? What would you do in the following situations? This quiz has no right or wrong answers, because each situation is unique. Your answers may be different from the ones given below, but they could be right under the circumstances.

1 Name Blame

Oops! Your classmate has asked you to use their new name. But you just called them by their old name. What can you do?

- Hope that they didn't notice.
- Apologize once, briefly, but don't make a big deal out of it.
- Make sure you use their new name in the next sentence.
- Make a mistake with your own name and comment that you are not doing well with names today.
- Commit to getting it right in the future. Practise in private at home.

2 Trash Talk

When you hear other people discussing another student's gender and putting them down, what can you do?

- Move away from the conversation.
- Let them know that you find what they are saying hurtful. Ask them to stop.
- Be clear with them that someone else's gender is none of their business.
- Report the conversation to an adult you trust at school (with or without names). Ask that all students get more training.

28

3 Girls' Room

You walk into the girls' washroom and see someone who you think doesn't really look like a girl. What should you do about this?

- Try not to stare at them.
- Ignore them.
- You're there to use the washroom. Go about your business and get out quickly.
- Act exactly as you normally would.

4 Temporary Teacher

You have a substitute teacher today. The teacher calls a classmate by their old name and insists they are a girl, even though they argue they are a boy.

- Forget it. The supply teacher will be gone soon.
- Make a point of using your classmate's current name in class.
- Ask if the supply teacher could call the vice principal to clarify the student's name.
- Say, "I don't know why it says that on the list. He's absolutely right about who he is."

5 Girl Power

Your school's girls' soccer team is defeated in the semi-finals by another school. Their team captain is a tall, muscular girl. Some of your teammates are insisting that she must be a boy and that's why they lost. They say they're going to make her prove she's a girl.

- Ignore them. They're all talk.
- The game's over. Tell them to move on.
- Point out that some girls are tall, some girls are not. Remind them that there's no point in worrying about a thing that can't be changed.
- Tell them that confronting the other girl would be worse than losing a game.
- Remind them that acting on what they are saying would be assault, and that's never okay.

Continues . . .

6 Info Block

There are no books about trans identities in your school library, and you are blocked from accessing information on the internet.

- Talk to the librarian. Suggest they unblock the word.
- Make suggestions of what titles you would like to see added to the school's library.
- Make use of the resources at the public library.
- Use the internet elsewhere. If you are concerned about other people knowing you are researching this topic, be sure to erase your browser history when you are done.

7 Dress Code

A friend confides that sometimes he likes to try on dresses and asks if you think that's okay.

- Change the subject.
- Tell your friend that it's not your thing, but you're okay with whatever makes him happy.
- Make sure your friend knows that you support him in his fashion choices.
- Ask him if he wants help in choosing colours and styles.

8 Foxy Fighter

You're watching mixed martial arts on TV with your dad. You're a big fan of Fallon Fox, but a competitor says she won't fight her because Fox is "really a man" and so is stronger. Your dad agrees that someone that used to be a man should not be fighting against women.

- Don't say anything if you're worried your dad might get angry.
- Tell your dad you like watching Fox fight.
- Point out that mixed martial arts' governing body has affirmed that Fallon Fox is a woman and can compete with other women.
- Tell your dad that cis women also come in different shapes and sizes. Suggest that performance has more to do with how you train.

9 What They Don't Know

Everyone has been really accepting of Thad's non-binary identity, except their older sister Corinne. When Thad's around, she always uses "they" and "them," but when they're not there, she doesn't. And you've heard her say some pretty transphobic stuff.

- You don't feel comfortable getting involved in Thad's family stuff, but you make sure you use "they" when you talk about Thad.
- You tell Thad and help them figure out what to say to their sister.
- Next time you hear Corinne say something, you say, "I'm really not comfortable hearing that, and I know Thad wouldn't be comfortable either."
- Next time you hear Corinne talking about Thad, you say "They, I know Thad would rather we call them they."

10 Unsocial Media

You see people posting pictures of a classmate online and calling her "tranny." You don't think she knows.

- Walk away, especially if you don't feel safe confronting them.
- Tell them that what they are doing is against the law.
- Take screen caps of what is happening and share it with an adult you trust (such as a parent or teacher).
- Tell your classmate and help her find out what to do about it.

More Help

Transphobia and gender stereotypes limit every one of us. It's important that we all work together to end them. Ask questions, challenge assumptions, be welcoming and friendly, stand up for your rights and the rights of others, and connect with others with similar goals. These are all great ways to start. Though it might not be easy to know what to do right away, here are some more resources to help you.

Help Organizations

Kids Help Phone: www.kidshelpphone.ca, phone 1-800-668-6868

LGBT Youth Line: www.youthline.ca, text (647) 694-4275, phone 1-800-268-9688

Trans Lifeline Canada: www.translifeline.org, phone 1-877-330-6366

Books and Resources

2 Spirited People of the 1st Nations: www.2spirits.com

Bending the Mold: An Action Kit for Transgender Students. Lambda Legal, 2008. www.lambdalegal.org/publications/bending-the-mold.

Beyond Magenta: Transgender Teens Speak Out by Susan Kuklin. Candlewick, 2015.

Beyond the Binary: A Tool Kit for Gender Identity Activism in Schools. Gay–Straight Alliance Network/Tides Center, Transgender Law Center and National Center for Lesbian Rights, 2004. www.gsanetwork.org/files/getinvolved/BeyondtheBinary-Manual.pdf.

Families in TRANSition: A Resource Guide for Parents of Trans Youth. Pride & Prejudice/Central Toronto Youth Services (CTYS), 2008.

The Gender Book by Mel Reiff Hill and Jay Mays. 2014. www.thegenderbook.com.

Gender Creative Kids/Enfants Transgenres Canada: www.gendercreativekids.ca.

Hello Cruel World: 101 Alternatives to Suicide for Teens, Freaks, and Other Outlaws by Kate Bornstein. Seven Stories Press, 2006.

Kids of Trans Resource Guide. COLAGE (Children of Lesbians and Gays Everywhere), 2010. www.colage.org/resources/kot.

Trans PULSE Project: www.transpulseproject.ca.

Fiction with trans characters

Being Emily by Rachel Gold. Bella Books, 2012.

George by Alex Gino. Scholastic, 2015.

Gracefully Grayson by Ami Polonsky. Disney-Hyperion. 2014.

Luna by Julie Anne Peters. Little, Brown, 2004.

Parrotfish by Ellen Wittlinger. Simon & Schuster, 2007.

Tomboy: A Graphic Memoir by Liz Prince. Zest Books, 2014.

Copyright © 2016 by j wallace skelton
Illustrations © 2016 by Nick Johnson

James Lorimer & Company Ltd., Publishers acknowledges the support of the Ontario Arts Council. We acknowledge the support of the Canada Council for the Arts which last year invested $24.3 million in writing and publishing throughout Canada. We acknowledge the Government of Ontario through the Ontario Media Development Corporation's Ontario Book Initiative.

Canada Council   Conseil des Arts
for the Arts   du Canada

ONTARIO ARTS COUNCIL
CONSEIL DES ARTS DE L'ONTARIO

Series design: Blair Kerrigan/Glyphics
Cover image: Shutterstock

Library and Archives Canada Cataloguing in Publication

skelton, j wallace, author
    Transphobia : deal with it and be a gender transcender / j wallace skelton.

ISBN 978-1-4594-0766-4 (bound)

    1. Transphobia--Prevention--Juvenile literature.
2. Transgender people--Identity--Juvenile literature.
3. Transgenderism--Juvenile literature. I. Title.

HQ77.96.S54 2016   j306.76'8   C2015-907200-X

James Lorimer & Company Ltd., Publishers
317 Adelaide Street West, Suite 1002
Toronto, ON, Canada
M5V 1P9
www.lorimer.ca

Printed and bound in Canada.
Manufactured by Friesens Corporation in Altona, Manitoba, Canada in November 2015
Job # 219244